D1466207

TEENS IN TURKEY

Teens in *Turkey*

by Alexandra Lilly

Content Adviser: David C. Cuthell, Ph.D.,
Director of the Institute for Turkish Studies,
Georgetown University

Reading Adviser: Alexa L. Sandmann, Ed.D.,
Professor of Literacy,
Kent State University

Compass Point Books ✦ Minneapolis, Minnesota

Compass Point Books
3109 West 50th Street, #115
Minneapolis, MN 55410

This book was manufactured with paper containing at least 10 percent post-consumer waste.

Editor: Julie Gassman
Designers: The Design Lab and Jaime Martens
Page Production: The Design Lab and Bobbie Nuytten
Photo Researcher: Eric Gohl
Cartographer: XNR Productions, Inc.
Library Consultant: Kathleen Baxter

Creative Director: Keith Griffin
Editorial Director: Nick Healy
Managing Editor: Catherine Neitge

Library of Congress Cataloging-in-Publication Data
Lilly, Alexandra
  Teens in Turkey / by Alexandra Lilly.
    p. cm.—(Global connections)
  Includes bibliographical references and index.
  ISBN 978-0-7565-3414-1 (library binding)
  1. Teenagers—Turkey—Social conditions—Juvenile literature. 2. Teenagers—Turkey—
  Social life and customs—Juvenile literature. 3. Turkey—Social conditions—21st century—
  Juvenile literature. 4. Turkey—Social life and customs—21st century—Juvenile literature.
  I. Title. II. Series.
  HQ799.T9S66 2008
  305.23509561—dc22   2007033090

Visit Compass Point Books on the Internet at www.compasspointbooks.com
or e-mail your request to custserv@compasspointbooks.com

Table of Contents

Ankara ✪

ATLANTIC
OCEAN

ATLANTIC
OCEAN

ICELAND

SCOTLAND
NORTHERN UNITED
IRELAND KINGDOM
IRELAND ENGLAND
WALES NETH.
BELGIUM
LUX.
FRANCE SWITZER.
ANDORRA
PORTUGAL SPAIN

Canary Islands MOROCCO TUN

WESTERN SAHARA ALGERIA

MAURITANIA MALI

SENEGAL
GAMBIA NIGER
GUINEA BISSAU
BRAZIL GUINEA
BURKINA
FASO
SIERRA LEONE BENIN
LIBERIA IVORY COAST NIGERIA
TOGO
GHANA

EQUATORIAL GUINEA
SAO TOME & PRINCIPE

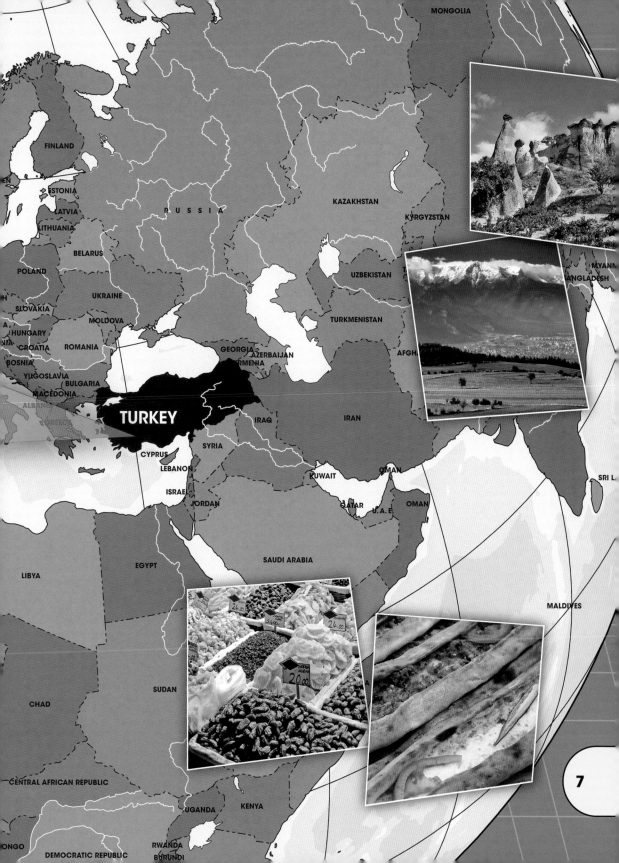

FINLAND

ESTONIA

LATVIA

LITHUANIA

RUSSIA

KAZAKHSTAN

KYRGYZSTAN

MONGOLIA

POLAND

BELARUS

UKRAINE

SLOVAKIA

MOLDOVA

HUNGARY

CROATIA

ROMANIA

BOSNIA

YUGOSLAVIA

BULGARIA

MACEDONIA

ALBANIA

GREECE

UZBEKISTAN

TURKMENISTAN

AFGH.

GEORGIA

AZERBAIJAN

ARMENIA

TURKEY

CYPRUS

LEBANON

ISRAEL

JORDAN

IRAQ

SYRIA

IRAN

KUWAIT

QATAR

U.A.E.

OMAN

OMAN

MYANM

BANGLADESH

SRI L.

LIBYA

EGYPT

SAUDI ARABIA

MALDIVES

CHAD

SUDAN

CENTRAL AFRICAN REPUBLIC

UGANDA

KENYA

ONGO

DEMOCRATIC REPUBLIC

RWANDA

BURUNDI

7

UNDER THE SUMMER SUN, TURKEY SIZZLES. At Ölü Deniz, on the southwestern coast, a family relaxes under a beach umbrella while a teenager tries sailboarding on the Mediterranean Sea. In Istanbul, a pair of teen girls board a ferry for a trip across the Bosporus, a narrow strait. The soft breeze off the water is a relief from the soaring heat. The girls stay in the shade and chat. A young man changes a tire on a car in his uncle's repair shop in Ankara, thankful for the fan blowing cool air in his direction. In the apricot orchards of Malatya, a girl and her mother pick basket after basket of fruit and quench their thirst with cups of fresh well water. A group of friends sprawl on the grass of the sports arena after soccer practice. Sweat pours off their bodies as they suck on slices of oranges.

Turkish teens make up nearly 22 percent of the country's population. They are much like young people everywhere. For some, summer is a vacation from school. For others, it is work. For all, it is a time for family and friends.

9

One of the government's top priorities is increasing the number of girls in school.

1

Getting an Education

ZIYA IS A 13-YEAR-OLD GIRL WHO GREW UP IN SOUTHERN TURKEY. The bright girl had to drop out of school when she was 9 in order to go to work. She spent the next four years laboring in a cornfield near Direklie. But her life recently changed, much to her excitement, happiness, and even disbelief. Thanks to a new government program, Ziya was able to go back to school. It was a dream come true.

Ziya lives with her parents and six siblings. Her father has been out of work on and off for years, so she had to work to help her family

survive. She seemed to have no future other than working in the fields. But in 2003, the Turkish government began a new program called *Haydi Kizlar Okula!* ("Hey, girls! Let's go to school!"). Parents would receive money for sending their daughters to school.

For many years, the Turkish government recognized that both boys and girls needed an education. Officials also knew that many

Haydi Kizlar Okula
hah-YEE-duh kihz-LAHR ah-KOO-luh

11

girls were kept home because their parents wrongly believed that the Qur'an, the Islamic holy book, forbade educating girls. However, Turkey's imams, who are high-ranking Muslim leaders, promote education for girls. Said one imam from the eastern province of Van, "It is a girl's right to go to school. A girl must be educated. Islam tells us this."

Some poor parents needed at least some of their children to work. The money helped pay for food, housing, or medicine. So while the boys continued at school, the girls earned money. One rural mother didn't see the need for education for her daughter. She said:

My husband and brother are working in Istanbul. I'm afraid to stay home alone. And I don't think my daughter really needs to go to school.

School records at the start of the program showed that 600,000 more boys attended school than girls. About 1 million primary-school-age girls didn't go to school. Leaders felt that had to change.

Teachers visit villages and speak to mothers about the importance of educating their daughters.

Teen Scenes

In Istanbul, two 16-year-old boys help change the oil on a car. They are working in their uncle's auto repair shop, training for their future. Both boys go to school in the morning and to work in the afternoon and on weekends. The money they earn helps their families pay rent on their apartments.

An 18-year-old girl has just gotten results from her Student Selection Examination. She scored well and has been accepted at Anadolu University in Eskişehir. The school has an intensive English language program, and this young woman is very good at languages. She hopes to become a translator for a Turkish business.

In a small town near Mersin, a 13-year-old girl helps her grandmother chop vegetables for the family restaurant. The restaurant is a pleasant café on a street corner near the shore. When school starts again, the teenager will not be going. She is going to work full time to prepare for a career as a chef. Her grandmother has cooked for the restaurant for many years, and this young girl will soon take her place. Her family has agreed to let her go to school two nights a week.

In Ankara, the capital, a 15-year-old boy studies the Qur'an. He is a student at an imam school and must keep up with his studies. Even during vacation, he continues his religious education, knowing that when school is in session he has a heavy workload.

Throughout Turkey, teens are seeing changes all around them. More girls are being given the opportunity for a better education and a brighter future. Boys train in vocations or hope to go to a university. Many teens will stay with their families, while others will branch out to new towns or cities. Regardless of what they choose to pursue, Turkish teens will always be linked to their families and hometowns.

Getting Around

One of the easiest ways to get around Istanbul is by using a *dolmus*, a shared taxi. For many students, it is the best way to get to school. Dolmus are blue-and-cream-colored minibuses that are cheaper than hiring a taxi and quicker than taking a bus. Unlike many means of public transportation, a dolmus will stop wherever a rider wishes to get off. Simply let your driver know. The driver pulls over, and out you go!

dolmus
dohl-MOOSH

Under Haydi Kizlar Okula, parents receive 25 to 35 Turkish liras (U.S.$19 to $27) each month for their daughters to go to school. The girls also receive food, school uniforms, and books. The government's goal is to reach 1.5 million families and get many more girls back in school. So far, more than 120,000 girls have enrolled in school.

Said Turkish President Ahmet Necdet Sezer:

In recent years, Turkish students have scored poorly on science exams. Government officials want to give teachers better training in science.

As both Nation and State, we must equip our children with the knowledge and skills required for the age in which we live, so that we don't fall behind the 21st century and so that we can improve the lot of our children.

The School System

Education in Turkey is required for eight years, from ages 6 through 14, but just over 10 percent do not attend. Public schooling is free, but families still have to buy school uniforms, books, and supplies. In other words, even a public education costs families money. School is open from September through June and usually lasts about eight hours a day.

For some children, schooling begins at age 4 with preschool. Elementary school goes from ages 6 to 11. Middle school is for children 12 to 14, and various forms of high school are for ages 15

Typical High School Subjects

Foreign languages

Math

Language arts

Science

through 17. Only elementary and middle school are required by law.

High school tries to prepare students for the future. Some students who hope to go to college attend a general high school, called a lycée. School is taught in Turkish, although English, French, and German are offered in many schools.

Vocational schools offer courses in technology, home economics, teacher training, health care, commercial studies, and agriculture. The government also sponsors schools that provide training to boys who wish to become Muslim religious leaders. About 10 percent of high school students attend *imam hatip okullari*, or imam schools, although most will need to find

imam hatip okullari
ih-MAHM hah-TIHP oh-KOOL-ahr-uh

different jobs. There are never enough places for so many imams. The curriculum in an imam school is divided into religious and nonreligious subjects. One-third of class time is spent on the Muslim religion, while two-thirds of the time is spent learning history, math, science, and languages.

Going to University

Students who wish to go to university must pass a Student Selection Examination. This is a comprehensive test given by the Center for Selection and Placement of Students. Test results determine whether the student can or cannot go to college and which college the student can attend. A high test score allows a student to study science or math. A student who scores low cannot become a professor or a doctor.

Each year, nearly 2 million students take the college admission test. There are only so many spaces for students who want to enter a university. The number of passing grades equals the number of available university spaces. In an average year, only 30 percent (roughly 600,000) of the test takers are able to go on to college at one of Turkey's more than 90 public and private universities.

Most students have tutors or take extra classes to prepare for the exam. Orcun, a student from Ankara, says:

The Student Selection Examination deprives us of many things at an age when we should be more social, more

INSTANBUL ÜNIVERSITESI

Istanbul University has five different campuses that serve a total of more than 68,000 students each year.

active. *I have university preparation courses six days a week. After eight hours of school, I have an extra four hours of courses, and I go home exhausted.*

Preparing for university is a full-time job. For those who fail to earn a spot, it is hard to find a high-paying job with just a high school diploma.

The job market is different for students who train for vocations such as auto mechanic, hairstylist, or electrician. Most vocational students can get work after they graduate, although most will not earn as much money as college graduates.

Education Reform

The government is constantly adding new programs that promote education. Major literacy campaigns are trying to reach girls and women between ages 14 and 44. In Turkey, men who can read and write far outnumber women with those skills. Illiteracy is the end product of keeping girls out of school. Literacy schools offer day and night classes and give women a chance to earn middle school and high school diplomas. Women who cannot read or write or who have no work skills have difficulty finding work and earning enough money to support their families.

Night school also offers opportunities for both men and women to learn new skills. Vocational training gives Turks a chance to get better jobs and earn more money. For many people who had to go to work as children, night school provides a future that did not exist before.

At textile schools, students learn how to create clothing, from dyeing the cloth to sewing a garmet.

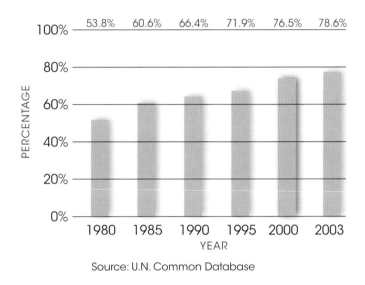

Growth in Female Literacy

53.8% 60.6% 66.4% 71.9% 76.5% 78.6%

PERCENTAGE

100%

80%

60%

40%

20%

0%

1980 1985 1990 1995 2000 2003

YEAR

Source: U.N. Common Database

The Turkish government also sponsors state boarding schools for children who live in remote areas where schools are too far away to travel to every day. The boarding schools are free and provide schooling, books, supplies, food, clothing, and housing for 280,000 students. The students even get spending money while they attend. The student boarding-school population is two-thirds male and one-third female.

Another education reform in the works is building more primary schools. Government leaders believe that local elementary schools in villages will draw more students, both girls and boys. They hope that the village school will become a community center and that education will then become a focal point for Turkish families.

Nearly 70 percent of Turks live in cities, which are growing rapidly.

2 From Country Fields to City Gecekondu

ACROSS TURKEY, PEOPLE ARE LEAVING THEIR COUNTRY HOMES TO MOVE INTO URBAN AREAS. Often they live temporarily with relatives while they look for work and homes of their own. Although the cities seem strange to them, the move from their village is made easier because of family ties. Their new homes might be small gecekondu, one-room buildings that literally are built overnight.

Though illegal, gecekondu are never torn down. In Ottoman times (1299–1922), a house built overnight could not be torn down, and the custom continues today. Nearly 65 percent of the buildings in Turkey are gecekondus. Each night, dozens of them appear in Istanbul, and most are built on government land. Many of

gecekondu
geh-jeh-CONE-doo

21

Turkey
Population density
and political map

Black Sea

BULGARIA

GREECE

İstanbul
Bosporus
Sea of
Marmara

Dardanelles

Bursa

Kütahya

Eskişehir

Ankara

ANATOLIA

İzmir

Ephesus

Aegean
Sea

Konya

Kayşeri

CAPPADOCIA

Samsun

Trabzon

GEORGIA

ARMENIA

AZ

Erzurum

IRAN

Van

Diyarbakir

Batman

TUR ABDIN

IRAQ

Öludeniz

LYCIA

Demre

Mersin

Adana

SYRIA

Mediterranean Sea

N
W   E
S

0   50   100 mi.
0   50   100 km

Population Density
(People per square km)

More than 200
100–200
50–99
10–49
Fewer than 10

these quick shelters have no water, no electricity, no toilets, and no heat. Eventually, the city may run electrical, water, and gas lines to these homes.

Living in a gecekondu is not as unpleasant as it sounds. Most have small gardens, and many gecekondu owners have jobs. People from the same region cluster together, creating a neighborhood atmosphere. Life is often upbeat in these communities.

City Life

Turkish cities are growing at a dramatic rate. About 320 people move into Istanbul every day. Likewise, 220 arrive in Izmir daily. Fifty years ago, most Turks lived in towns and villages. A 2005 population study showed that 67 percent of Turkish citizens live in cities. Turkey's major cities are Istanbul, Ankara, Izmir, Bursa, and Adana.

Most city dwellers live in apartments. Some buy their apartments, while others rent. Most Turkish cities are modern. People have televisions, VCRs, and CD players. They store food in refrigerators, heat it in microwave ovens, and clean the plates in dishwashers.

Driving in Turkish cities can be a challenge like no other. Traffic laws are seemingly ignored. Drivers cross yellow lines to pass slow-moving vehicles. Whenever there is someone in the way, drivers blow their horn. A couple of toots means "hurry up." If you don't,

the driver behind you will pass whether the road is clear or not. Main highways are filled with trucks and buses. Those in small cars must beware: They might get run off the road. One other thing—you have to watch out for tractors, horse carts, and the occasional camel. They, too, share the right to travel on Turkey's highways.

City workers are employed in industry, finance, and services.

Straddling Two Continents

Turkey lies in both Europe and Asia. The European portion, to the west, is known as Thrace. It covers only 3 percent of Turkey's total area but is home to more than 10 percent of the total population. Thrace is separated from the Asian portion, or Anatolia, by the Bosporus strait, the Sea of Marmara, and the Dardanelles, another narrow strait.

Istanbul is home to famous mosques, such as the Hagia Sophia and the Blue Mosque.

Turkey's economy ranks 21st in the world in industrial production, but third among Muslim nations. Top industries refine oil, manufacture chemicals, and make iron and steel. The textile industry produces fabric by machine and rugs by hand.

Istanbul is Turkey's largest city, with an estimated 10 million people. Unofficial population estimates are much higher. Knowing the exact number is nearly impossible, since so many people live in illegal housing. The only city in the world to lie in two continents, Istanbul straddles the border between Europe and Asia. On the European side, businesses flourish, museums attract tourists, and passersby admire ancient monuments. Cross the Bosporus, and you are in Asia. This side of Istanbul is mostly residential. Because of its key location, Istanbul serves as a transportation hub serving European and Asian cities.

Istanbul blends ancient and modern on every corner. More than 2,500 years old, the city has high-rise apartments that back up against old-style street markets. Clusters of modern shops overlook ancient buildings, like the Hagia Sophia mosque and the Topkapi Palace.

Though Istanbul is Turkey's largest city, it is not the government center. Until 1923, Ankara was a sleepy village where most people raised angora (Ankara) goats. Then Turkey's leader, Kemal Atatürk—who is better known simply as Atatürk—made Ankara the capital city and the seat of government. Because it is a relatively new city,

compared with Istanbul, Ankara has broad, tree-lined streets and many public parks. Between 3 million and 4 million people live in Ankara, and most work for the government or provide services for government workers.

Lying on the western coast, Izmir has been called the "pearl of the Aegean Sea." For years, pollution made the bay on which the city sits smell awful. Since 1997, the bay has been cleaned up. Now Izmir is a delightful seaside city with sidewalk cafés. It is home to about 2.5 million people year-round, and thousands more tourists visit during the summer months.

Shopping on a String

In some Istanbul neighborhoods, grocery stores set up business on the ground floor of apartment buildings. The residents have an easy way of shopping. They lower baskets with grocery lists on ropes from their apartment windows. The market fills the orders, and the purchasers haul the baskets up. These convenient shops are called *bakkal* and often stay open as late as 10:00 P.M.

bakkal
bahk-KAHL

A young woman knits while she watches over the family goat herd. Rural days are filled with work, making it a good idea to combine tasks.

Rural Life

Rural families often live in small villages and commute to cornfields and other farms for work each day. They prefer the social life in town to living in a lonely, remote farmhouse. Men, women, and children are all likely to take part in fieldwork.

Of the Turkish women who work, 58 percent work on farms. In fact, 78 percent of all fieldworkers are women. Ninety percent of those who work in the hazelnut orchards are women or girls. When they're not working on the farm, women do housework. The honor of the family depends heavily on the cleanliness of the home. Windows are washed at least once a week and, sometimes, every single day.

Homes may be large or small, but most have a front room for guests, a kitchen and eating area, and bedrooms.

The family room may be another room, like a den, or it may simply be a large, eat-in kitchen. The front room is always spotless and is used for guests only. Village women invite friends for tea in their front parlor. When the family gets together, they use another room.

Rural life is more traditional than city life. Fathers are considered the "boss" of the household. Children in rural villages are more likely to work after school or quit school early to work full time. Even if they attend school, they are still expected to help with the work of planting and harvesting. Girls provide the extra money needed for the family to survive. Besides going to work early in life, girls who live in villages will probably marry younger than those who live in cities.

Rural Wanderers

Along the coastal region of Turkey, groups of nomads called *yörüks* set up camp in open fields. Yörüks are shepherds, goatherds, and weavers. They move their flocks to the mountain plateaus in spring and summer, and return to the

yörüks
yoh-ROOKZ

Colorful rugs fill a fixed tent home of nomads in central Turkey. Because it has been staked to the ground, the tent offers more protection from the elements.

coastal pastures in the winter.

Nomads once packed everything they owned on the backs of camels and traveled with their flocks. They lived in open-air tents made of goat hide, camel hide, or wool. Today nomads keep permanent houses along the coasts and in the mountains, shifting with their flocks. There are still groups that travel by camel (although many prefer pickup trucks) and control their flocks with the help of dogs.

Many nomadic clans continue to weave rugs, which feature colors and patterns traditional to their region. The rugs are frequently sold at street markets. Yörük men may be seen in black shaggy goat-hair capes during winter months, although they usually wear jeans and a sweatshirt under their capes. Women are more likely to wear traditional clothing, including baggy trousers, short jackets, and scarves.

Food & Drink

"Eating is a communal ceremony in Turkish culture and tradition," says writer Meral Kaya. Meals are a time to bring families together and welcome guests into the home. Whether in the city or the country, the key to Turkish life is hospitality. Visitors are always made welcome. Ensuring that guests are comfortable is expected of every host. Guests are always offered the best seat and the best food available.

Breakfast in Turkey is usually feta cheese, tomatoes, olives, cucumbers, and sometimes a hard-boiled egg. The meal is accompanied by bread with jam or honey. Tea is the beverage of choice to start the day. Grown in the Black Sea coastal region, tea is the most popular drink served at home. Modern Turks also drink coffee, fruit juices, soft drinks, and bottled water. For teens who attend school, breakfast is almost always prepared by their mothers.

A typical breakfast is served on the floor, as is common when dining at home.

A Nation of Tea Drinkers

Most Turks drink tea with their meals. Although Turkey may be known for Turkish coffee, its people consume 120,000 tons (108,000 metric tons) of tea every year. Tea is brewed in a large urn, called a samovar. It is served in tulip-shaped glasses, with two sugar cubes and no milk. Popular tea flavors include apple, linden, rose hip, mint, and lime flower.

In a city, the best place for lunch is a *lokanta*, a type of cafeteria. These restaurants serve a variety of *sulu yemek*, or "juicy food," which is stew. It may feature chicken, beef, lamb, or fish, and a variety of vegetables. Eggplant is popular, as are tomatoes, onions, green beans, and peas. Though fast-food

lokanta
loh-KAHN-tuh
sulu yemek
shoo-LOO yeh-MEHK

chains such as McDonald's and Wendy's can be found in cities, most teens prefer traditional dishes.

Bread is a must with every Turkish meal. Flat bread, or pita, is used to sop up gravies or sauces. Thicker, whole-grain breads are served with cheese or soup, which Turks eat at any time of the day. Both yogurt soup with rice and fish soup are favorites that can be homemade or purchased at restaurants called çorbaci.

In the afternoon, Turkish people often enjoy a snack. Apple tea with sugar and a variety of pastries are commonly offered to visitors. While women entertain guests in the parlor, men prefer to meet in the coffee shop. A local coffeehouse provides more than just a small cup of very strong coffee. This is a place for men to meet their friends, read the newspaper, talk about politics or business, or watch football (soccer) on television. This is no place for women or children—it's men

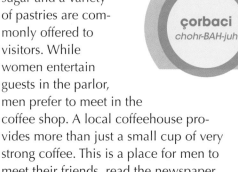

çorbaci
chohr-BAH-juh

Turkish Pizza

Similar to pizza, with its bread crust and toppings, Turkish *pide* is a popular dish. Pide is long and narrow and rolled up at the edges. The dough is topped with white or Cheddar cheese plus meat, spinach, or cooked egg. There is no tomato sauce— and definitely no pepperoni.

pide
pih-deh

Pide is considered Turkish fast food.

Delicatessens serve a wide variety of Turkish dishes featuring fresh fruits and vegetables.

only! In contrast, tea shops welcome all comers—male or female, adult or child.

As for the evening meal, dinner begins with hot or cold appetizers called *meze*. Stuffed pastry, salads, and *dolma* are offered to whet the appetite. Dolma is basically anything stuffed—zucchini, eggplant, grape or cabbage leaves, mussels, peppers, and clam-

shells. The fillings usually include pine nuts or pistachios, currants, onions, olives, minced meat, or a variety of other goodies.

The main course may be a kebab—grilled pieces of meat, fish, and vegetables on skewers. Kebabs arrive on a bed of pilau, a Turkish rice dish. Most grilled foods have received ample marinating with olive oil and lemon juice—two staples of the Turkish kitchen.

meze
meh-ZEH
dolma
DOHL-mah

Turks love their desserts, which may come from the pastry shop or the pudding shop. Baklava—filo dough baked with nuts and honey—comes in an array of shapes, all with whimsical names such as Lady's Navel and Twisted Turban. One of the most interesting puddings is *asure*, a combination of beans and dried fruits.

Lokum is a delicious candy commonly called Turkish Delight. This sweet treat comes in a variety of flavors, including rose, lemon, hazelnut, and pistachio. Turkish Delight is a jelly in a fine coating that is made from sugar,

Courtyard cafés in urban areas provide serene areas for lunch or tea.

An unknown Englishman liked lokum so much he shipped the candy to England and gave it the name Turkish Delight.

A Candy Revival

In the novel, *The Lion, the Witch, and the Wardrobe*, by C.S. Lewis, the character Edmund treasures lokum when it is given to him by the White Witch. First introduced to Europe in the late 1700s, Turkish Delight became popular again when the movie *The Chronicles of Narnia: The Lion, the Witch and the Wardrobe*, based on the Lewis novel, was released in 2005.

flavoring, cream of tartar, cornstarch, and water.

Of course, weight-conscious Turks often skip the pastry and candy and finish their dinners with fresh fruit. Locally grown watermelon, apricots, cherries, figs, and pomegranates are available in street markets.

If a meal is delicious, a gracious guest offers compliments to the chef, whether in a home or in a restaurant. The typical expression that says everything was delicious is simple: Put the tips of your thumb and fingers together, then bounce your hand up and down. A tip for the server is always welcome, as is a gift of flowers or chocolate when visiting someone's home.

Turkish teens tend to have close relationships with their families, especially with their parents.

3 The Value of Family

WHETHER IN THE CITY OR THE COUNTRY, FAMILY IS THE FOCAL POINT OF MOST TURKISH LIVES. Turks are extremely social people. They love their families, their neighbors, their communities, and their nation.

National loyalty extends to national symbols. Turks are offended by jokes about their country, the national anthem, the flag, and the country's founder, Atatürk. Foreigners or guests are never encouraged to offer opinions about Turkish politics, political leaders, or items in the news. While these topics may be discussed among Turks, they are off bounds for outsiders.

In the neighborhood or community, Turks are always ready to lend a helping hand. Earthquakes have plagued the nation. Turks are quick to provide housing, food, clothing, and more to those in need. It is expected that neighbors will put up extra guests who come to town for a family wedding or funeral.

As cities grow, families are not able to reach out to others as easily. Today many city families are made up of just mom, dad, and the kids. They may not see their extended families often, but responsibility to the family does not lessen with distance. The eldest son will still be expected to look after his parents when they are old. The government gives aid, such as a pension, to elderly people. But an elder son is truly the Turkish retirement program. He will provide a home and care for his parents when they become too old to work.

Family Roles

The roles of father, mother, and children are fairly rigid in Turkey. Father is the head of the household, and what he says goes. Father is expected to earn the bulk of the family money and provide a home. If the family lives with or near relatives, it will be the father's family they are close to. Fathers are expected to work outside the home, and few do any housework.

In Turkey, keeping house is women's work, even if the mother works full time. Mothers may put in eight-hour days at offices or stores, then do the shopping and the laundry. And they still have to cook and clean house at home each evening. As a rule, daughters will help; sons do not. The family's honor is closely related to the household and its tidiness. If guests arrive unexpectedly,

Memleket & Hemsehri

Two ideas dominate the relationships between Turks. *Memleket* deals with a person's hometown, and *hemsehri* deals with a person's fellow countrymen. People who are born in a town consider that place home, even if they moved away as infants. That town is the center of family ties, and those ties do not lessen if a Turk is far away. Their sense of memleket never leaves them. People from small towns who live in cities look for others from that town to form their social network. They help others from their area get jobs or build gecekondus. However, when a Turk speaks of Turkey, particularly to foreigners, it is always the feeling of hemsehri, pride in Turkey, that comes through.

memleket
mehm-LEH-keht
hemsehri
hehm-SHEH-ruh

An elderly Turkish woman milks a goat. Because women do both domestic and farm work, men in rural areas are often more dependent on the woman than vice versa.

the front room must be spotless, with tea and treats available to serve.

The Role of Women

Though women still fill the traditional roles of caregivers and housekeepers, they enjoy many more freedoms than Turkish women of the past. Many years ago, upper-class adult women lived in a harem. This was a secluded area in a home that was dedicated to, and run by, the women of the household. Men, even male relatives, never entered the harem. Here, young women learned arts and crafts, music, and reading and writing. Local interpretation of the Qur'an dictated that women appear fully covered in public. But within the harem, the women could be uncovered. Women in the harem enjoyed a

Harems were home to both upper-class women and lower-class servants.

comfortable, relaxed atmosphere.

As free as women were within the harem, they had few freedoms outside it. They could not hold jobs for pay, vote, or hold political office. Few women owned anything but their clothes, jewelry, and other personal possessions. Young girls could be wed without their agreement in marriages arranged by their fathers.

Great changes came for women after Atatürk became Turkey's leader in 1923. Atatürk set up a secular nation, a country that was not ruled by religious leaders. He also established a new civil law. In doing this, Atatürk freed women from their past. On paper, women were given the same rights men have. The minimum age for marriage for women was set at 15, although it has since been raised to 17. And girls had the chance to go to school—the same school that the boys attended. This was a major adjustment for Turkish families.

Then in 1934, women received the right to vote in Turkish national elections. It is hard for people now to

What to Wear

Since women achieved equal civil rights in Turkey in 1926, many have chosen to dress like European women. Working women wear the latest business suits, silk blouses, and high heels. Teenage girls are expected to dress modestly, but T-shirts, sneakers, and jeans are common. For dress-up occasions, European-style clothing is the norm. That means dresses for the girls, and shirts with collars and ties for the boys. Many observant Turkish Muslim women (perhaps 30 percent of the female population) dress in *tesettür*, a headscarf and light cover-all topcoat, when going out in public. In Turkey, how a woman dresses is her choice. If women prefer to be veiled in public, that's fine. If women at beach resorts choose to wear bikinis, that's fine, too.

tesettür
TEH-seh-tur

Dress is varied among Turkish teen girls.

Though mothers take the lead on childcare, fathers also enjoy close relationships with their children.

realize what a tremendous step this was. Turkish women could vote when women in France and Italy could not.

Though the laws changed, attitudes took more time to change. In most homes, husbands were still the boss. Wives who wanted to work outside the home had to ask permission from their husbands. This is no longer true.

Today 9 million Turkish women work outside the home. They hold positions as teachers, secretaries, clerks, nurses, doctors, pilots, army officers, and police officers. In 1993, Tansu Çiller, an economist and politician, became the first female prime minister of Turkey and served for three years. Turkish women have come a long way from the harem.

Parental Love & Support

Family size depends mostly on where the family lives. City families tend to have one, two, or three children. Rural families, particularly in farm districts, have larger families. They need the children to help work on the farm and tend livestock. Children are the delight of every family. They are raised primarily by their mother, with a bit of help from grandma. Strict rules and regulations are not common in Turkish households. Children are rarely scolded—never in public. When they misbehave, it is said that they are simply acting like . . . well, children. Although children do not have to follow many rules, they are expected to show respect to their elders.

Turkish parents do not hire baby sitters so that mom and dad can enjoy a night out alone. Instead, parents usually bring their children with them when they go out. Children are welcome in most restaurants, hotels, museums, and

Showing Respect

In Turkey, last names are not commonly used when addressing another person. Instead, Turks use a variety of titles that show respect, friendship, or family ties. When talking to someone older, it is common to use *amca* (uncle), *teyze* (aunt), *bey* (sir), or *hanim* (lady). Teenagers or young adults are called *agabey* (big brother) or *abla* (elder sister). Teachers are called by their first names plus *hoca* (teacher).

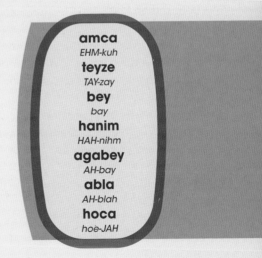

amca
EHM-kuh
teyze
TAY-zay
bey
bay
hanim
HAH-nihm
agabey
AH-bay
abla
AH-blah
hoca
hoē-JAH

Friends spend time together shopping, playing sports, or just hanging out.

other public places. Older brothers and sisters entertain the younger ones. Babies are handed from sister to brother, bounced on knees, and treated with gentleness and love.

Because children spend so much time with their parents, it is not surprising that many friendships come from ties to the family. Teens are often friends of the children of their parents' friends. They may also make friends at school or in their neighborhood.

When it comes to dating, teens are more likely to go out with someone they already know well. But if their parents are more liberal, they might be more likely to date outside of this familiar social circle.

Like almost everything else in Turkey, what is acceptable for dating couples in the big cities is very different from what is acceptable in small towns and villages. In the cities, teens get together for dates or in groups and go to concerts, sporting events, movies, teahouses, or shopping centers. In rural areas, teen social life revolves more around the family. Teens are less likely to date and more likely to enter into an engagement and marriage based on family rather than personal wishes.

Minorities in Turkey

As in other countries, minorities in Turkey have different experiences than the majority population. In the southeastern region of Turkey, many people are Kurds. This ethnic group, which makes up just 20 percent of the population, has its own language, style of dress, and customs. Kurds also live in Iraq, Iran, and Syria.

Some Turkish laws did not allow Kurds to use their language or follow certain customs. As recently as 1980, a Kurd in an open market could be fined 5 piastres for every Kurdish word spoken in public. Since a sheep was worth 50 piastres, the fine was serious.

As a result, the Kurds felt they had been oppressed as a minority. A group called the PKK, a militant rebel organization, fought against the government to earn greater freedoms for Kurds. One major complaint was that Kurds could not speak Kurdish in schools or have Kurdish television or radio stations.

In recent years, the government has relaxed these rules, and problems between Kurds and the Turkish government have eased somewhat. However, there is still a feeling that many Kurds

Each year, Kurds celebrate Newroz, a festival to mark the first day of spring.

In the 1970s and 1980s, thousands of Suriyanis moved to the West because of economic troubles. Many are now returning to their homeland.

would like to separate from Turkey and have their own country.

Another minority, the Laz, are Caucasians. They trace their heritage back to the Caucasus region of central Europe. The Laz, like the Kurds, have their own language. Unlike the Kurds, the Laz have spread throughout Turkey, mainly to the cities. Many Laz enter into business, and some run restaurants.

About 50,000 Turks belong to an ethnic group called the Suriyanis. This minority is found mostly in Tur Abdin, in southeastern Turkey. Once, Tur Abdin was the seat of the Syrian Orthodox Church.

The town had 80 monasteries. Priests and monks flocked to the region to study and pray. Today only three monasteries remain. Suriyani men often work as jewelers and are skilled at working with both gold and gemstones.

About 40,000 to 50,000 Armenians live in Turkey, mainly along the northeast border with Azerbaijan. Although they are citizens of Turkey, Turkish Armenians tend to separate themselves from other Turks. They attend their own churches and publish Armenian books and magazines, but have the same rights as other Turkish citizens.

Jews have found a safe haven in Turkey for more than 2,400 years. According to the Bible, Noah landed his ark on the top of Mount Ararat, in present-day Turkey's Taurus Mountains. For centuries, Jews looked to Turkey as a homeland. Jewish migration to Turkey reached a height in 1492, when many Jews were forced to leave Spain. They traveled the length of the Mediterranean Sea and established themselves as a part of the Turkish community.

Fewer than 20,000 Jews remain in Turkey. They live mainly in Istanbul, Izmir, Ankara, and several smaller cities. Despite the differences between Muslims and Jews, Turks respect their Jewish citizens. Although Turks accept Jews as part of their culture, Islamic groups outside Turkey do not. In 2003, agents from al-Qaida, an Islamic terrorist group, bombed two synagogues in Istanbul. Twenty-five people died in the attack, and about 300 were injured. After a lengthy police effort, the government charged more than 70 people in the bombings, including several al-Qaida leaders.

The Neve Shalom Synagogue reopened less than a year after the front of the synagogue collapsed in the 2003 bombing.

45

Families gather together to celebrate honored times, such as weddings.

4 Honoring Special Times

A TEENAGE BRIDE WELCOMES HER FRIENDS AND FEMALE RELATIVES TO HER HOME. Tonight is her "henna night." Tomorrow she will be married, even though she just turned 17.

Henna night is a tradition that honors the bride. The bridegroom's family brings dry henna, a type of dye, to the bride's home. There is a great deal of chatter, gossip, and excitement before the bride takes the seat of honor. But as she enters the room, the mood becomes more serious. The young girls in attendance sing a song to the bride: "You will leave your mother and father and never see them again." The henna is broken into pieces in a silver or copper dish and mixed with water to make a brick-red paste.

Before the henna is applied to the bride's skin, women place gold or coins in the bride's hands. Then her hands are painted with the strong dye. If she agrees, her feet and hair also may be dyed. She is blessed with good wishes for her future life as a wife and mother. After the henna ceremony, the older women leave, and the bride and her friends party all night.

For some girls, marriage is an arranged event. In today's

Turkey, this means that the parents approve of a possible match between a young man and woman. The bride and groom meet and get to know each other before the wedding is planned. The marriage will take place only if the young man and woman agree.

In Turkey, a wedding is never just a religious event; only civil marriages are legal. The couple must answer questions before a local government official. The actual ceremonies are quick, but the celebrations may last for several days.

Half of all couples in Turkey have both civil and religious ceremonies. Forty percent of marriages have only civil ceremonies. And in some rural areas, girls agree to marry in the mosque only and may not realize their marriage is not legal.

Milestones in Life

Every family milestone is a cause for celebration. This includes births, deaths, and every major life event in between. When a couple is expecting a child, the family is delighted. The future paternal

The average Turkish bride is 23 years old. The groom is 26.

grandmother gives her daughter-in-law a gold bracelet. The birth draws family members from throughout the country. Both the new mother and the child get gifts—particularly if the baby is a boy.

In Anatolia, the southern peninsula of Turkey, families often celebrate a birth by planting a tree. If the baby is a girl, the tree will be chestnut, mulberry, or apple. Poplar and pine trees are most often planted in honor of a boy.

The choice of a name for the new baby is very important. Turkish names have meanings. A child may be named for the time of the birth—Rafak (Dawn), Bahar (Spring), or Ramazan (the month of Ramadan). Other names refer to flowers (Songul means "last rose"), emotions (Meryem means "beloved"), or virtues (Emine means "reliable"). In rural villages, the parents may select a name and tell the local imam. The imam holds the child facing Mecca,

What's in a Name?

Common Turkish Boys' Names	Common Turkish Girls' Names
Abdullah	Ayse
Ahmet	Büsra
Ali	Dilara
Emre	Fatma
Furkan	Hatiçe
Hasad	Irem
Hüseyn	Merve
Kemal	Sema
Khan	Smine
Mehmet	Umay
Mustafa	Zeynep
Okan	
Osman	

Circumcision ceremonies hail from Ottoman times. It is one of the few Turkish customs that was not affected by Atatürk's modernization.

Islam's holy city. He speaks a phrase from the Qur'an into the child's left ear and the chosen name into the right ear. The child's name is now official.

Boys are honored by their community when they are circumcised. All Turkish Muslim boys between 2 and 14 years old have a circumcision ceremony. This is a step toward manhood and a cause for celebration. Family and friends gather for the event, which turns into a huge, multiday party.

In a village, the boy is paraded through town like a king on horseback or in a cart. Musicians move through the crowds, beating drums and playing clarinets. The honored son wears a special costume that includes a cape and a hat, and he carries a scepter. Of course, presents are given. Gold coins are attached to pillows with red ribbons and offered to the boy to represent the gifts he will take with him as an adult.

Death and burial are as much a part of life as birth. Once again, the family gets together. When a person dies, the body is laid on a bed.

Bathing Ritual

A *hamam* is a public Turkish bath, and bathing is both a ritual and a celebration. Since medieval times, Turkish villages and cities have had public baths. While the bath is a place to get clean, it is also a place to relax and gossip. Old and young, rich and poor, everyone uses the hamam.

hamam
hah-MAHM

Men and women bathe at different times, and all major life events are celebrated by bathing. Brides bathe before their weddings, often enjoying food and music. On a baby's 40th day, the child is bathed at the hamam. Even after a death, bathing becomes important. The hamam ceremony of mourning was a ritual established to help wash away sorrow.

On a regular basis, a Turkish bath brings together people from many walks of life. It is, in its own way, a celebration of life. The hamam not only cleans the body, but it also revives the spirit.

During a Turkish bath, bathers lie in a hot room before splashing down with cold water. They then wash themselves, receive a massage, and go to a cooling room to end the bath.

Women bathe a deceased woman's body. Men are bathed only by men. The dead person's head is positioned to face Mecca. The big toes are tied together, and arms are laid beside the body. Burial takes place as soon as possible.

The body is wrapped in a white cloth and laid on a green cloth in a coffin. An imam leads the family and friends in prayer. By tradition, the imam asks the people whether the deceased person was worthy, and they always answer, "He was good. May God bless him." It is wrong to speak badly about someone who died.

Family and friends go to the cemetery. The body will be buried only in the cloth wrapping, not the coffin. The body lies on its right shoulder, facing Mecca. It is considered a holy act to assist in a burial, so many mourners help cover the body with dirt. The death is remembered with readings from the Qur'an on the 40th and 52nd days after the death, and in some rare occasions on the third and seventh days, too.

The Muslim Majority

The *muezzin* calls out from the tower of the local mosque, *"Allah-u Akbar,"*— "God is great." In the mosque below, in local shops, and households, the faithful bow toward Mecca and recite their prayers. Devout Muslims follow the five pillars of Islam, one of which is praying five times a day. More than 99 percent of Turks are Muslim.

The majority of Turkish Muslims are Sunni Muslims, although there are other Muslim sects, including Shi'ites and Sufis. Most Turkish Sunni Muslims have a fairly liberal view of Islamic life.

> **muezzin**
> *moo-eh-ZIHN*
> **Allah-u Akbar**
> *ah-LAH-oo ahk-BAHR*

The Five Pillars of Islam

To be considered a devout Muslim, one must meet these requirements:
- Recite the creed: "There is no god but Allah and Muhammad is his prophet."
- Pray five times daily.
- Observe the annual monthlong fast.
- Give alms to the poor.
- Make a pilgrimage to Mecca at least once during one's lifetime.

Because Alevis have done away with many Islamic practices, they sometimes face discrimination from more traditional Muslims.

They are more accepting of other religions and beliefs than those who follow stricter, more traditional beliefs. However, there are some groups of Sunnis that follow a very strict version of Islam. Some of these Muslims would like to have a religious-run government. Most Turks believe that government and religion should be kept separate.

The differences between Sunni and Shi'ite Muslims go back to shortly after the death of the Muslim prophet Muhammad more than 1,300 years ago. When Muhammad died, Muslims needed a religious leader. The Sunnis chose to follow Caliph Hasan. The Shi'ites followed Muhammad's daughter Fatima and her husband, Ali.

Twenty million Turkish Muslims are Alevis. Alevism in Turkey follows a moderate view of Islam. Women have equal status with men, and often both sexes pray together. Prayer meetings are held in meeting houses rather than in mosques.

Sufism is yet another sect of Islam. The Sufis in Turkey follow the teachings of the 13th-century poet Mevlana, who lived in Konya. During the festival honoring the death of Mevlana, Sufi followers participate in the Sema ritual. Dervishes—holy men—dress in long, flowing white robes and cone-shaped hats. They greet each other, and verses are read from the Qur'an. Each dervish lifts one arm toward heaven and God,

Dervishes do not whirl as entertainment, but viewing their ceremony has become a tourist attraction in Turkey.

while the other reaches down toward the earth. The dervishes whirl around and around, their circles representing the connection of the soul to God. The goal of whirling is to reach unity with God and may last an hour or more.

Religious Holidays

The dates of Muslim holidays change every year because they follow the Islamic calendar. Although the Islamic calendar has 12 months, each month has fewer days than the months of the

Gregorian calendar, which is used in most countries. Basically, the Muslim calendar year is completed in 11 Gregorian calendar months.

For everyday purposes, Turkey uses the Gregorian calendar. Because Islamic calendar months are shorter, the dates of holidays "move up" about a month each year on the Gregorian calendar. Thus, Ramazan (or Ramadan), the monthlong fast, may come in January one year, December the next, and November the year after.

The most important religious holiday in Turkey is Kurban Bayrami, known elsewhere as Eid al-Adha. It is a four-day feast that honors the story of Abraham and his willingness to sacrifice his son to God. Instead, Abraham is told to sacrifice a ram, and Turks follow this tradition. They sacrifice lambs and donate the meat to the poor.

Ramazan is a monthlong fast during which adult Muslims do not eat or drink during the day. It is perfectly all right to rise early and eat breakfast, called sahur, before dawn. In many villages, drummers march through the streets announcing the time the fast will begin that day. A message runs along the television screen announcing the dawn and dusk times of each day so people will know when to start and end their fasts.

At the end of the day, Muslims break the fast with a feast called *iftar*.

sahur
sah-HOOR
iftar
if-TAHR

This nightly feast is a time for women to show off their cooking skills. For weeks before, famous chefs demonstrate special iftar recipes on television. This is also a time for charity. Muslims donate money and food to provide iftar feasts for the poor. Towns sponsor jugglers, fireworks, puppet shows, and folk music concerts during this period.

Ramazan officially ends with Seker Bayrami (or Eid al-Fitr), a three-day feast. This is the "sugar" holiday, and adults give sweets and cash to children. It is a time to visit families, even if they are distant. Families also visit the graves of relatives. Even businesses get into the spirit of the

Jolly Old St. Nick

Every year thousands of pilgrims flock to Demre, Turkey, the birthplace of Saint Nicholas. Early in the 1950s, Turks realized that the figure known as Santa Claus or Father Christmas was their own St. Nicholas, the bishop of Myra in the fourth century. St. Nicholas is the patron saint of bakers, pawnbrokers, sailors, children, Greeks, and Russians. His feast day is held on December 6.

holiday, with owners giving employees and customers boxes of chocolates.

Public Holidays

Most public holidays in Turkey center on the actions of Atatürk during the Turkish War of Independence (1919–1923). Gazi Mustafa Kemal Pasha (1881–1938) was an army officer, a war hero, and a revolutionary leader. He became the country's first president after the war and took the name Atatürk (Father Turk) in 1934. Atatürk established Turkey as a republic and formed the Grand National Assembly of Turkey.

National Sovereignty and Children's Day is April 23. It is the anniversary of the day the Grand National Assembly was established. Schools hold parades, and children recite poems in Atatürk's honor. At home, in schools, outside business buildings, and on the streets, people display Turkish flags with pride. Children may go house to house ringing doorbells for candy, similar to trick-or-treating in other countries. Youth and Sports Day (May 19)

Public Holidays

New Year's Day—January 1

National Sovereignty and Children's Day—April 23

Youth and Sports Day—May 19

Conquest Day—May 29

Navy Day—July 1

Victory Day—August 30

Republic Day—October 29

Atatürk Commemoration Day—November 10

Students take part in ceremonies to celebrate Youth and Sports Day in May.

recalls the start of the War of Independence. Stadiums might sponsor sporting events and folk dancing.

Victory Day, August 30, honors the day when the War of Independence ended and foreign rulers were removed from Turkey. This is a military event and honors the army, navy, and air force. At night, Turks move through the streets with flashlights or candles to remember the sacrifices of those who fought for freedom. October 29, Republic Day, brings another patriotic celebration. Turks recognize the day by displaying flags and listening to political speeches.

Public holidays are a time for national pride and patriotism. Turks love their country. It is an honor to take part in any of the parades and a duty to fly the nation's flag. This is all part of the intense Turkish feeling stated in the saying, "*Ne mutlu Türküm diyene*"—"How happy is he or she who can say, 'I am Turkish.'"

Ne mutlu Türküm diyene
neh moot-LOO toor-KOOM dih-YEH-neh

Many of the job choices in Turkey are handed down through generations. Teens are likely to do the same type of work as their parents did.

5

Required to Work

CHILD LABOR IS A SERIOUS CONCERN FOR TURKEY'S GOVERNMENT. About one-fourth of children ages 10 to 17 have jobs. And children as young as 5 or 6 work in addition to, or instead of, going to school.

The welfare of working children is important. There is no question that children would rather be out playing than earning a living. Education, too, is threatened when time spent learning must become time spent working. Many Turkish children, however, have no choice. Nearly 40 percent of children who work do so to add their money to the family income. In many cases, the father can only find part-time work, and the mother must care for the rest of the children at home. About 20 percent of working children are helping out in family businesses.

Whether working alongside parents in a shop or cornfield or learning a trade in an apprenticeship, many Turkish teens have found their way in the working world.

The Grand Bazaar

Every day, 250,000 to 400,000 shoppers pour into Istanbul's Grand Bazaar, one of the largest and oldest covered shopping districts in the world. Established in the mid-1400s, the Grand Bazaar claims to have 3,000 shops on 58 connected streets. This ancient "mall" is divided into two major sections, and shops are grouped by the types of goods they sell.

Shoppers can buy just about anything they need in the bazaar shops: clothing, shoes, jewelry, food, carpets, fabric, brassware, tile, pottery, luggage, and furniture. The market is open every day except Sunday. Shoppers wear comfortable shoes—this shopping trip requires plenty of walking.

The Grand Bazaar is a major attraction for foreign tourists.

Investigating Child Labor

In 1992, Turkey joined a United Nations-based effort to control and monitor child labor. In effect, Turkey began a program against child labor. The first task was to find out where children worked. Next, how did this work affect their health? What were the working conditions? Did work prevent a child from gaining an education?

Many children work part time, helping their families after school in stores or restaurants. In open markets, children often mind the stalls, make sales, and handle money. Children do these jobs after school, and their work helps support the family. Jobs in which children help in the family business did not worry the government as much as jobs that were dangerous or that prevented children from going to school.

The government set up a program for inspecting places where children worked. During a two-year period, the inspectors were able to withdraw or prevent 4,000 children from being in unsafe work situations. Furniture factories and leatherworks jobs were found to be particularly dangerous.

Inspectors discovered that children working in furniture factories regularly handled dangerous chemicals and machinery. They breathed in chemical fumes and wood dust. They were exposed to loud noise with no earplugs to protect their hearing. Many children working in this type of environment suffered accidents that resulted in

Though many jobs are not a danger to children's health, the government identifies all types of child labor as a risk to young people.

Street children often become addicted to drugs, compounding their problems.

permanent injuries. Others suffered from weak or damaged lungs. Officials removed children from the worst of these places and recommended fans, breathing masks, and safety guards for machines in others.

Factory work was not the only area where child labor was common. In farm districts, many girls worked in corn or wheat fields, or picked figs, apricots, or nuts. Farm families needed help for planting and harvest. Many families hold traditional values, and the fathers do not see any need to send their daughters to school. The program to encourage parents to let their daughters go to school and

to pay back the families for the lost income has proved successful.

Turkey also has more than 3.8 million street children. These children have been abandoned by their parents and live on their own. They beg on the streets or sell tissues or pieces of food to earn money. Many children in these situations are forced to steal in order to survive. They roam through open markets in search of items they can grab and eat or snatch and sell.

This is a serious problem that the government is trying to address. Various organizations both within and outside of Turkey are working for a solution as well. Nejat Kocabay, an official working to eliminate child labor, noted that combining the efforts of various groups was required to save street children. He said:

We should be proud. In our efforts, we integrate children's social environment and many organizations cooperate with us. The model used in Turkey aimed to minimize the time children spend on the streets by providing social, cultural, and educational opportunities.

Learning Skills

More than a million Turkish children have entered an apprentice program. One teenager, Hosni, is learning to be a jeweler, and the work is demanding. He lives with the family of a master jeweler and gets his housing and food as part of his pay. What little money does come his way he sends home to his parents. Eventually, he, too, will be a master jeweler and will earn a good living from this skill.

In the meantime, Hosni's life is very busy. He rises early to study before work. At the jewelry shop, he is learning how to set gemstones into gold mounts. After work, he grabs a quick meal and heads off to school. When he finishes his apprenticeship, he will have a school diploma and a skill.

Apprentices, like 13-year-old salesman Erdem Karatas, gain valuable on-the-job training that often leads to a career.

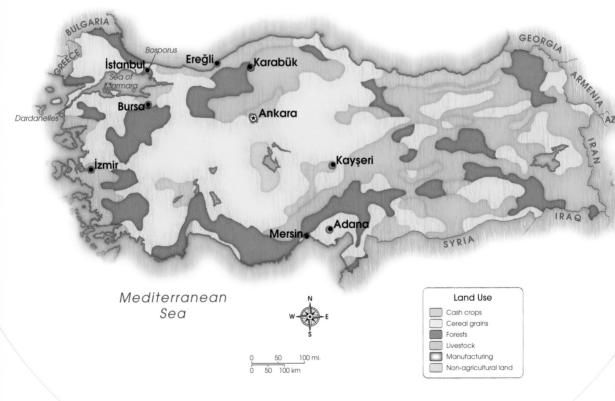

Turkey
Land use map

Black Sea

BULGARIA

GREECE

Bosporus

İstanbul

Ereğli

Karabük

GEORGIA

ARMENIA

Sea of Marmara

Dardanelles

Bursa

Ankara

AZ

İzmir

Kayşeri

IRAN

Adana

Mersin

IRAQ

SYRIA

Mediterranean Sea

N
W   E
S

0   50   100 mi.
0 50 100 km

Land Use

Cash crops
Cereal grains
Forests
Livestock
Manufacturing
Non-agricultural land

Division of Labor

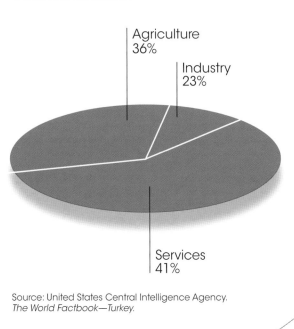

Agriculture
36%

Industry
23%

Services
41%

Source: United States Central Intelligence Agency.
The World Factbook—Turkey.

Seventy-seven percent of Turkey's working children—mostly girls—work in agriculture. Many work during the day, then attend night school. Some primary schools have two shifts to include all the students, and girls are being dismissed from work early to attend.

Turkey is one of the top 10 producers of fruit, wheat, and cotton in the world. The nation also produces large quantities of vegetables, apricots, nuts, and tea. Common grain crops include barley, oats, corn, maize, millet, and rice. Beans, peas, and lentils are mainly grown in the central regions of Turkey.

Turkish farmers also raise industrial crops, which produce a product rather than food. Among the main industrial crops are sugar beets and tobacco.

Although girls work in the fields, fathers will pass the land they own on to their sons. Farmers, fishermen, and restaurant and shop owners expect their sons to work beside them when they become adults. This is the traditional way in which families live and work together. It makes no sense to leave a business to a daughter, because she is expected to marry and move in with her husband's family. But as Turkey changes from a rural, farm-based economy to an urban, services-based economy, many sons are no longer following in their father's footsteps. The farmer's son is becoming a banker; the fisherman's boy is deciding to become an engineer.

For generations, women in certain areas of Turkey have woven rugs for a living. Turkey is known for producing some of the finest handcrafted rugs in the world. The skill is passed from mother to daughter; the two sit side-by-side working at the loom.

A weaver must learn to dye wool yarn following methods used for centuries. The rug's pattern is passed down through a family for more years than the living weavers can recall. The pattern is geometric, and the rug is called a *kilim*. Weave, knot, cut … weave, knot, cut. Their hands make quick, sure motions as the rug's pattern is slowly revealed. The weaving process seems endless, with each rug having more than a million hand-tied knots.

kilim
keh-LEEM

For children who live in Turkey's coastal and resort cities, summer jobs provide added spending money and funds for school supplies. Turkey has a flourishing tourism industry. Teens help provide services for tourists. With more tourists, hotels fill up, restaurants serve more meals, and street markets thrive. Teens who want to work can usually find employment doing laundry, cleaning, selling ice cream, making hotel beds, or running the family's fruit and vegetable cart.

A Stint in the Army

No matter what career a Turkish boy pursues, he can expect to serve in the military. Turkish law requires all men between 20 and 41 to serve in the military, and service is considered a sacred duty. At 20, Turkish men receive "call up" papers telling them when and where to report for duty. In rural areas, this is cause for a celebration. Friends and family gather to send off the soldier-to-be, giving him gifts of money and food for the journey.

Turkish men who have a limited education serve 15 months as privates

Earning Tips

Many Turkish employees receive minimum wages on the job. As a result, those who provide services expect tips, known as bashish. Workers who expect tips include those in restaurant service, taxi drivers, bellboys, tour guides, barbers, car park attendants, and Turkish bath attendants.

Some military members get their start by attending military high schools. Young cadets wear T-shirts with portraits of Atatürk.

ATAM İZİNDE

in the army. For a university student, military service can be delayed up to one year. University graduates become reserve officers and train for four months, then serve for 12 months. Turks who have been living abroad and return to Turkey when they are adults must still do their military service.

There is no acceptable reason for refusing to serve other than physical disability. In 1998, a famous Turkish pop star, Tarkan, was on tour in France and failed to show up for his required service. Tarkan was labeled a deserter and faced a prison sentence for failure to follow Turkish law. In February 2000, he returned to Turkey to fulfill his military service. Failure to do so might have meant loss of citizenship. In another incident, a member of Turkey's parliament was accused of submitting a false medical report to avoid his time in the army. The government minister was put on trial and faced jail. In Turkey, service is an honor, and failure to serve is a disgrace.

Like teens everywhere, young people in Turkey are happy just hanging out with one another.

6

Loving Life, Having Fun

THE TURKISH GOVERN-MENT HIGHLY VALUES THE COUNTRY'S YOUNG PEOPLE. Officials want to make sure that teens are happy and healthy. Article 58 of the Turkish constitution reads, "The State shall take necessary measures to protect youth from addiction to alcohol, drug addiction, crime, gambling, and similar vices, and ignorances." Leaders interpret the law to mean that the government should provide safe and, of course, fun activities. Four national agencies work to ensure young people have plenty of opportunities for leisure.

Government-sponsored youth centers provide a place for teens to learn arts and crafts, play sports, and receive guidance for dealing with problems. More than 22,000 young people are active in more than 100 youth centers. The government also sponsors summer camps that give teens a chance to relax, escape from work and studies, and participate in their favorite sports.

Whether through a government program or a spur-of-the-moment plan, Turkish teens love to take time out to relax. Traditional music, shopping, and oil wrestling are just a few favorites.

Playing Okey

okey
oh-kay

Okey is a popular Turkish game played with a set of 106 wooden tiles. Tile faces are painted with numbers 1 to 13 in red, yellow, green, or black. There are two of each number in each color, making eight tiles per number. Two special tiles, called false jokers, are blank.

The game is similar to the card game rummy, but far older. The object is to be the first to form a hand that consists entirely of sets of equal numbered tiles and runs of consecutive tiles of the same color. Players draw and discard tiles to build the winning hand.

Okey is almost always played with four players.

Fun from the Past

As children, Turkish teens listened to folk tales, sang folk songs, and watched puppet shows. In the past, folk music was never written down. Instead, it was passed from singer to singer. There are several types of folk music, based on the origin. The music of the whirling dervishes is eerie, reedy, and hypnotic. Ottoman military music is performed by bands and played with drums, cymbals, and bells.

Performing arts are designed to entertain, teach, and honor the past. In villages, special holidays, such as Republic Day or a wedding, feature plays. A *meddah* is a one-act drama with a narrator who must play the roles of many characters in the play.

meddah
MEHD-duh

Dramas do not attract children as much as puppet shows do. Shadow puppets are human or animal figures cut from leather and painted. A light source from behind casts a shadow on a white screen. When the light comes on, the children hush. The play is about to begin. Most shadow plays are comedies. One character, in particular, has won the hearts of Turkish children and adults: Karagöz. Along with his friend Hacivat, Karagöz gets into all sorts of silly situations. Their actions have kept Turks laughing for centuries.

Folk dances are performed at weddings and on other festive

Young puppeteers take apprenticeships from masters to learn the art.

71

occasions, such as national holidays. The Black Sea dance, called *horon*, is danced only by men. The dancers dress in black outfits with silver decorations. They link arms and move to the rhythms of the *kemence*, a stringed instrument. In the Spoon Dance, gaily dressed men and women twirl to lively music, tapping out the beat with wooden spoons in each hand.

horon
HOE-rohn
kemence
keh-MEHN-jeh

The Arts

Turkey is a living museum. Across the country, ancient ruins, Roman baths, centuries-old churches and mosques, open-air theaters, and countless statues can be found everywhere. Some of these precious artworks are preserved in museums, such as the Mosaics Museum or Topkapi Palace in Istanbul. Other treasures are seen in mosques, such as the Selimiye Mosque in Edirne or Haghia Sophia in Istanbul. Still other wonders are at the end of a rock-strewn walk, such as the Temple of Trajan in Begama, the stone heads of Mount Nemrut, or the underground cities of Cappadocia.

The Iznik region, in Turkey's northwest area, once produced ceramics of such beauty that they were prized around the world. Fine painted and glazed pottery was produced by Iznik artisans for centuries. The cobalt blue-on-

Palace Like No Other

In the 1470s, Mehmet II built the remarkable Topkapi Palace. Topkapi is a maze of gardens, courtyards, and stunning rooms. Today it is a museum that presents the art, culture, and history of Turkey for every visitor to enjoy. Begin in the kitchen, where china collections represent the great treasures of China and Japan. Crystal as delicate as a butterfly's wing is displayed beside cauldrons that once cooked enough food for 12,000 guests. Silken robes, jeweled daggers, and centuries-old tapestries re-create the culture of Turkey over the past 500 years.

King Antiochos I, who ruled from 69 to 36 B.C., had his tomb built at Mount Nemrut. Several statue heads remain as ruins.

white floral tiles can be seen in Topkapi Palace. Iznik ceramic art stopped being produced in the late 1600s, but it can be found in museums and mosques throughout Turkey. Excellent copies are also available at street markets in Kütahya, where many glass and china products are made.

Let's Go Shopping

Shopping is a favorite winter pastime for many Turks. Modern handicrafts can be found at local street stalls and art galleries. Smart shoppers haggle over prices, which can be high for truly fine work. The best buys are definitely at the street markets. Brass work and hand-beaten copper make

73

Since the late 1990s, outlet centers have become popular shopping spots for Turks.

popular products such as lamps, pots, plates, and even lunchboxes.

Needle lace consists of delicate, floral patterns that have been crocheted in silk and attached to linens. Many brides and their mothers work countless hours to produce needle lace for the bride's first household. These fine linens are also available for a price. The finer the work, the higher the price.

Handmade jewelry comes in every style and every price range. Gold and silver are sold by weight and then fashioned into earrings, necklaces, and bracelets. The selection is extraordinary, and since so many jewelers set up shop in the Grand Bazaar, prices are reasonable.

On the rare day off without the family, teens in major cities in Turkey head to the mall. Shopping malls are great places to window shop, check out the latest fashions, and have a snack in the food court. Turkish teens know that the mall is the place where they can be comfortable with their friends and even pick up a bargain on sale.

Music to Turks' Ears

Turks of all ages love music, and Turkish teens listen to everything from opera to pop. Radio stations play a wide range of music styles. Jazz, rock, and pop are teen favorites, but true Turkish music must include *sanat*, *fasil*, and *arabesk*.

Sanat is classical music featuring drums and wind and stringed instruments. During the Ramazan fast, concerts of sanat

sanat
sah-NAHT
fasil
fah-SEEL
arabesk
ah-rah-BESK

Turkish teens pick up their favorite music recordings at area superstores.

Cirit Games

In ancient Turkey, cavalry soldiers competed in a sport called *cirit*, played mostly by riders on Arabian horses. Cirit is a game of fake combat, much like medieval tournaments. Two teams (seven to 10 players) are each armed with a 3-foot (90-centimeter) stick. Teams line up across from each other, 140 yards (128 meters) apart. One rider races forward and hurls his stick, then rides away. The opponent pursues the first rider, trying to hit him with his thrown stick. The teams alternate, with each player throwing his stick. A hit counts for six points; making a horse veer off-course is worth three. Today's cirit games are played every Sunday from May to September.

cirit
JEE-riht

music are featured. Many of these concerts are held in open-air or state-operated music halls. Some are also featured on television so the music can be enjoyed by a wider audience.

Fasil is semi-classical Turkish music that is best listened to in person. There are clubs that feature fasil music, and concerts are held in small towns. The music blends the sounds of drums, clarinets, and stringed instruments. Fasil has a folk-song quality and is usually performed with dancers.

Arabesk is the kind of music people might hear while riding in a taxi or an elevator. It features sad, heartrending ballads. Arabesk artists are the pop culture heroes of Turkey. They have a tremendous following, and their albums sell in the millions.

As with American pop music, Turkish pop got its start in the late 1950s. In the early pop days, Turkish singers produced English-language versions of songs by Americans Frank Sinatra, Elvis Presley, and Doris Day. Today Turkish artists write and produce their own music. Popular singers include Tarkan and Sezen Aksu. Their music mirrors popular trends in Europe and the United States, mixing hip-hop, heavy metal, reggae, and rap. Turkish artists combine European sounds with Indian sounds, lay on a bit of Arabic and a touch of folk music, and wind up with a sound all their own.

Becoming a hit means being heard on radio and seen on television.

Pop Royals

Both Tarkan and Sezen Aksu have been given royal titles by Turkish pop fans. Tarkan is often called the Turkish Prince of Pop, and Aksu is called the Queen of Turkish Pop.

Dance and pop music star Tarkan is popular throughout Europe. His 1999 single, "Simarik," made him an overnight success in European clubs and led to the release of his self-titled album that year. His full name is Tarkan Tevetoglu. Although he is Turkish, he was born in Alzey, Germany, and lives in New York City.

Turkish singer and songwriter Sezen Aksu was born Fatma Sezen Yildririm in Denzil, Turkey, in 1954. She spent her youth in Izmir, near Istanbul. Aksu is not only a singer but an actress in several Turkish musicals. In 2005, she was featured in the documentary film *Crossing the Bridge: The Sound of Istanbul*, performing the song "Istanbul Hatirasi."

Tarkan was named after a popular 1960s Turkish comic book character.

Turkey has its own talent-scout television program called *Turkstar*. The show is based on the popular British music show *Pop Idol*. Talented singers are scouted in all the major cities, and a jury of famous musicians judges the results. The show is a big hit with teens, whose TV viewing also includes movies, sports, shopping, and music television channels. Turks can watch Fox Sports, the Discovery Channel, and Animal Planet on local Turkish channels.

Get Fit!

Turks participate in sports at every level: spectator, amateur, and professional. Playing sports is actually written into the Turkish constitution, which requires the government to "develop the physical and mental health of Turkish citizens of all ages and encourage the spread of sports among the masses." There are more than 2,500 sports facilities and more than 6,000 sports clubs in Turkey, with only 261 privately run.

The Directorate General of Youth and Sports, an official agency that reports directly to the prime minister, organizes sports programs in 81 provinces. Each province has its own sports network, complete with coaches, referees, and fans. The range of interests covers 37 sports federations—everything from track and field to tae kwon do, archery to auto racing, and billiards to badminton.

Many of the sports followed in Turkey are familiar to teens around the world: basketball, football (soccer), and boxing, for example. Others are quite different. Oil wrestling, or *yagli gures*, is a Turkish sport that is not well known anywhere else. It is one of the nation's most popular sports. Each summer, wrestlers meet on the open fields at Edirne for the oil wrestling championship. The athletes smear themselves with olive oil, which makes it hard to get a good grip. The event is a mix of tradition, sport, and party, with music, lamb roasts, and a crowd of fans cheering on their favorite wrestlers.

yagli gures
yah-GLUH goo-REHS

For those who don't care for men wrestling, there is always camel wrestling. As part of this winter event, the camels are decorated and paraded through the streets of Aegean villages before the matches. Proud camel owners boast that their beasts can beat any others, and they challenge other bull camel owners to meet them. The actual events are less brutal and more comic than spectators might expect, but the fans come out to cheer anyway. Two bulls face each other, charge, and butt heads. Sometimes, one knocks the other over. The real excitement comes when a bull decides to look for better competition and charges into the crowd!

Sports attract both male and female athletes, and Turkey boasts international medal winners from both sexes. Turkey won its first Olympic championship with Yaşar Erkan in wrestling at the 1936

Getting the camels to fight is not a problem; male camels naturally fight for their females during mating season.

Berlin Olympic Games. In 1998, the Eczacıbaşı women's volleyball team won the European Cup. A year later, Hülya Şahin took a gold medal at the European Boxing Cup for Women, held in Sweden. As with most nations, sports heroes are honored and cheered as national treasures. This is especially true in Turkey, where national pride and sports success are closely linked.

Pack Your Bags

Since Turkish students have three months off for the summer, most families choose to go on vacation at that time. Many head to the shores to beat the heat. Luckily, Turkey has beaches on the Black Sea, the Aegean, and the Mediterranean. Turkey's fabulous crystal-blue waters and clean sandy beaches draw tourists from around the world, but Turks know the

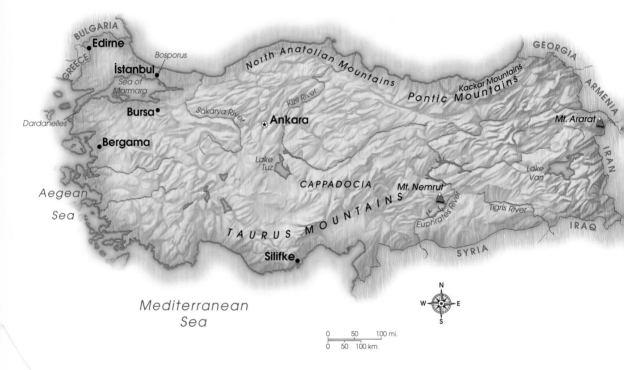

Turkey
Topographical
map

Black Sea

BULGARIA
GREECE
•Edirne
Bosporus
İstanbul
Sea of
Marmara
Dardanelles
•Bursa
•Bergama

North Anatolian Mountains
Kizil River
Sakarya River
★ Ankara
Lake Tuz

GEORGIA
Pontic Mountains
Kackar Mountains
ARMENIA
Mt. Ararat
IRAN
Lake Van

CAPPADOCIA
Mt. Nemrut
Euphrates River
Tigris River
IRAQ
SYRIA

Aegean
Sea

TAURUS MOUNTAINS
Silifke•

Mediterranean
Sea

N
W—E
S

0   50   100 mi.
0   50 100 km

Turkey's beaches provide favorite teen spots for sand and surf.

best places to go. Many Turkish families own or rent beach houses to get away from Istanbul or Ankara.

There teens can soar over the water on a parasail, rent a sailboat for an afternoon, or just sunbathe on a lounge chair. The water is warm and clear, and scuba diving might reveal some hidden treasure. Hundreds of ancient jars and bottles have been scooped up off the floor of the Mediterranean Sea. Or teens can don a snorkel and mask and watch the multicolored fish that collect around shipwrecks along the coast.

Some people can't get away to the shore, but they can take advantage of Turkey's many rivers, streams, and lakes. People escape the heat by setting up aluminum chairs and tables in quiet streams. They'll open a book, drink some ice-cold fruit juice, and relax while cool water trickles over their bare feet. Whitewater rafting is a wet and wild roller-coaster-like ride available in Silifke, a town on the coast, and on several Turkish rivers in the Kaçkar Mountains. It, too, provides a break from summer heat.

When winter comes, vacationers head to the mountains. About 60 percent of Turkey lies more than 3,300 feet (1,000 meters) above sea level. Winter cold means snow on the mountains. Turkey first became interested in skiing when Russian soldiers introduced the sport during their World War I occupation. Turkey's first ski club was established in Bursa in the 1930s. Today more than 20 ski resorts dot the mountains. Both skiing and snowboarding are becoming more popular.

Looking Ahead

TURKISH TEENS LIVE AND PLAY WHERE ANCIENT CIVILIZATIONS ONCE FLOURISHED. They live in Bursa, where caravans once rested after months of travel along the Silk Road from China. They attend school in Ephesus, the town conquered by King Croesus of Lydia in 560 B.C. They buy spices for their mothers at the Spice Bazaar in Istanbul, where, for centuries, women have bought herbs and spices displayed in baskets.

Today Turkish teens can go to school and hope for a good career. Others have jobs in cities, working to help support their families. Teens watch television, play video games, and listen to music on MP3 players. Some wear jeans; others cover their bodies with long robes. Teens cheer for their favorite soccer teams or play for youth teams. Their lives are varied and full.

For most Turkish children, the focal point of daily life is family. As they grow and pursue different interests, they still maintain that connection. Their link to family is also a link to their hometown or region, and, finally, to their country. No matter where they go in their lives, a Turk's greatest pride is being Turkish.

Official name: Republic of Turkey

Capital: Ankara

People

Population: 71,158,647

Population by age group:
0–14 years: 25%
15–64 years: 68%
65 years and over: 7%

Life expectancy at birth: 72.88 years

Official language: Turkish

Other common languages: Kurdish, Dimli (or Zaza), Azeri, Kabardian

Religion:
Muslim (mostly Sunni): 99.8%
Other (mostly Christians and Jews): 0.2%

Legal ages:
Alcohol consumption: 16
Driver's license: 18
Employment: 15 (13 for light work)
Marriage: 17
Military service: 20
Voting: 18

Government

Type of government: Republican parliamentary democracy

Chief of state: President elected by the Grand National Assembly of Turkey for a seven-year term

Head of government: Prime minister, appointed by the president

Lawmaking body: Turkiye Buyuk Millet Meclisi (Grand National Assembly of Turkey), 550 seats, elected by popular vote for five-year terms

Administrative divisions: 81 provinces

Independence: October 29, 1923 (established as a country following the fall of the Ottoman Empire)

National symbols:
Flag: Called "moon star"
Emblems: Star and crescent

Geography

Total area: 312,232 square miles, (780,580 square kilometers)

Climate: Temperate; hot, dry summers with mild, wet winters; harsher in the interior

Highest point: Mount Ararat, 17,048 feet (5,166 m)

Lowest point: Mediterranean Sea, sea level

Major rivers: Tigris, Kizilirmak, Sakarya, Euphrates

Major landforms: High central plateau (Anatolia); narrow coastal plain; North Anatolian Mountains, the Pontic Mountains, and the Kaçkar Mountains

Economy

Currency: Turkish lira

Population below poverty line: 20%

Major natural resources: Coal, iron ore, copper, chromium, antimony, mercury, gold, barite, borate, celestite (strontium), emery, feldspar, limestone, magnesite, marble, perlite, pumice, pyrites (sulfur), clay, arable land, hydropower

Major agricultural products: Tobacco, cotton, grain, olives, sugar beets, pulse, citrus fruits, livestock

Major exports: Apparel, foodstuffs, textiles, metal products, transportation equipment

Major imports: Machinery, chemicals, semi-finished goods, fuels, transportation equipment

Historical Timeline

Hunter-gatherers make flint spearheads

Constantinople (Istanbul) is founded by emperor Constantine

Alexander the Great claims southeastern Turkey

| 20,000 B.C. | 17,000 | 9000 | 334 | 130 | A.D. 330 | 1453 |

Early Stone Age settlement exists in Antalya

Modern humans settle in Anatolia

Ottomans seize Constantinople and rename it Istanbul

Rome conquers much of western Asia, including Turkey

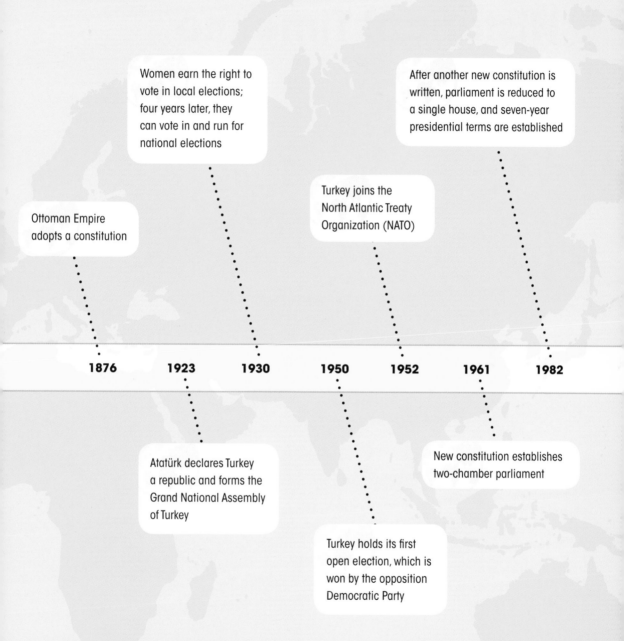

Women earn the right to vote in local elections; four years later, they can vote in and run for national elections

After another new constitution is written, parliament is reduced to a single house, and seven-year presidential terms are established

Turkey joins the North Atlantic Treaty Organization (NATO)

Ottoman Empire adopts a constitution

1876   1923   1930   1950   1952   1961   1982

Atatürk declares Turkey a republic and forms the Grand National Assembly of Turkey

New constitution establishes two-chamber parliament

Turkey holds its first open election, which is won by the opposition Democratic Party

Historical Timeline

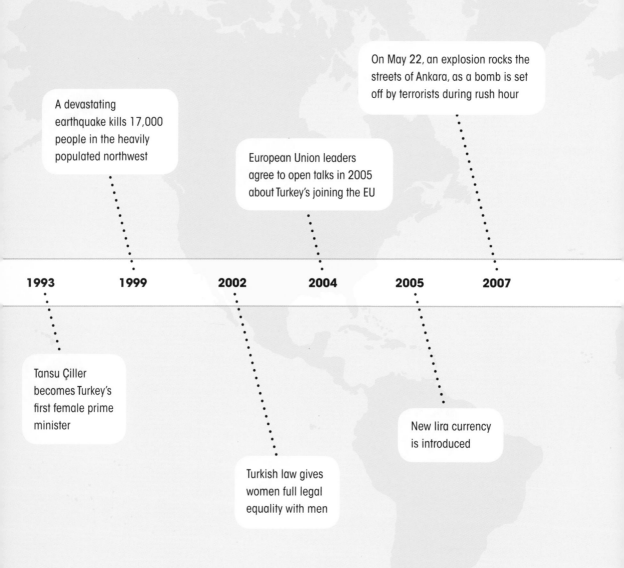

A devastating earthquake kills 17,000 people in the heavily populated northwest

On May 22, an explosion rocks the streets of Ankara, as a bomb is set off by terrorists during rush hour

European Union leaders agree to open talks in 2005 about Turkey's joining the EU

1993　**1999**　**2002**　**2004**　**2005**　**2007**

Tansu Çiller becomes Turkey's first female prime minister

New lira currency is introduced

Turkish law gives women full legal equality with men

Glossary

apprenticeship | the time a person works under a skilled professional in order to learn an art, craft, or skill

circumcised | had the foreskin of a penis surgically removed

commercial | relating to business

imam | high-ranking Muslim leader

Islam | religion founded by the prophet Muhammad; followers of Islam are called Muslims

liberal | not bound by traditional customs or beliefs

literacy | the quality or state of being able to read

mosque | Islamic place of worship

Muhammad | Arab prophet and founder of Islam

Ottoman | relating to the Turkish Ottoman Empire, its rulers, its citizens, or its government officials; the Ottoman Empire was founded in 1300 and ruled until after World War I

Qur'an | the holy book of Islam

residential | relating to a place or area where people have houses or apartments

secular | not controlled by a religious body or concerned with religious matters

sovereignty | political independence or freedom from outside political rule

Additional Resources

FURTHER READING

Fiction and nonfiction titles to further enhance your introduction to teens in Turkey, past and present.

Bagdasarian, Adam. *Forgotten Fire*. New York: Laurel-Leaf Books, 2002.

Hiçyilmaz, Gaye. *Against the Storm*. Boston: Little, Brown, 1992.

Walker, Barbara K. *A Treasury of Turkish Folktales for Children*. Hamden, Conn.: Linnet Books, 1988.

Bodnarchuk, Kari. *Kurdistan: Region Under Siege*. Minneapolis: Lerner Publishing Group, 2000.

Cornell, Kari A., and Nurcay Turkoglu. *Cooking the Turkish Way*. Minneapolis: Lerner Publishing Group, 2004.

Kherdian, David. *The Road from Home: A True Story of Courage, Survival, and Hope*. New York: HarperCollins Publisher, 1995.

ON THE WEB

For more information on this topic, use FactHound.
1. Go to www.facthound.com
2. Type in this book ID: 0756534143
3. Click on the *Fetch It* button.

Look for more Global Connections books.

Source Notes

Page 12, column 1, line 8: "Going Door-to-Door in Turkey for Girls' Education." UNICEF. 29 Dec. 2005. 8 Aug. 2007. www.unicef.org/infobycountry/Turkey_30668.html

Page 12, column 2, line 4: Ibid.

Page 15, column 1, line 1: *The First Children's Forum Ankara, 2000.* UNICEF. 2000. 8 Aug. 2007. www.unicef.org/turkey/pdf/cr18.pdf, p. 3.

Page 16, column 2, line 35: Ibid., p. 14.

Page 28, column 1, line 25: Meral Kaya. "Turkey." *Teen Life in the Middle East.* Ed. Ali Akbar Mahdi. Westport, Conn.: Greenwood Press, 2003, p. 216.

Page 47, column 1, line 19: Jenny B. White. "Two Weddings." *Everyday Life in the Muslim Middle East.* 2nd ed. Eds. Donna Lee Bowen and Evelyn A. Early. Bloomington: Indiana University Press, 2002, p. 70.

Page 63, column 1, line 5: "Turkey Sets the Standard on Helping Street Children." *Turkish Daily News.* 29 June 2006. 8 Aug. 2007. www.turkishdailynews.com.tr/article.php?enewsid=47386

Page 69, column 1, line 8: "The Constitution of the Republic of Turkey." Chapter Three. Hellenic Resources Network. 8 Aug. 2007. www.hri.org/docs/turkey/part_ii_3.html#article_58

Page 78, column 1, line 18: Ibid.

Pages 84–85, At a Glance: United States. Central Intelligence Agency. *The World Factbook—Turkey.* 19 July 2007. 9 Aug. 2007. https://www.cia.gov/library/publications/the-world-factbook/geos/tu.html

Select Bibliography

Aksin, Sina. *Turkey From Empire to Revolutionary Republic*. New York: New York University Press, 2006.

All About Turkey. 1996–2007. 9 Aug. 2007. www.allaboutturkey.com

"Calendars Through the Ages: The Islamic Calendar." WebExhibits. 9 Aug. 2007. http://webexhibits.org/calendars/calendar-islamic.html

"The Constitution of the Republic of Turkey." Hellenic Resources Network. 8 Aug. 2007. www.hri.org/docs/turkey/

"Discover Turkey: Government." 1995–1996. 9 Aug. 2007. www.turkishnews.com/DiscoverTurkey/government

Ergener, Rashid (Resit). *About Turkey: Geography, Economy, Politics, Religion,and Culture*. Boulder, Colo.: Pilgrims Process, 2002.

The First Children's Forum Ankara, 2000. UNICEF. 2000. 8 Aug. 2007. www.unicef.org/turkey/pdf/cr18.pdf

"Going Door-to-Door in Turkey for Girls' Education." UNICEF. 29 Dec. 2005. 8 Aug. 2007. www.unicef.org/infobycountry/Turkey_30668.html

Kaya, Meral. "Turkey." *Teen Life in the Middle East*. Ed. Ali Akbar Mahdi. Westport, Conn.: Greenwood Press, 2003.

McPherson, Charlotte. *Turkey: A Quick Guide to Customs and Etiquette*. Portland, Ore.: Graphic Arts Center Pub., 2005.

Republic of Turkey. Grand National Assembly of Turkey. 9 Aug. 2007. www.tbmm.gov.tr/english/english.htm

Republic of Turkey. Ministry of Culture and Tourism. 9 Aug. 2007. www.kultur.gov.tr/

Seferoglu, S. Sadi. "Education in Turkey." 9 Aug. 2007. www.columbia.edu/~sss31/Turkiye/education-tr.html

Swan, Suzanne. *Turkey*. London, England: Dorling-Kindersley, 2003.

"Turkey." *Encyclopaedia of the Orient*. 8 Aug. 2007. http://lexicorient.com/e.o/index.htm

"Turkey." Governments on the WWW. 20 Oct. 2001. 9 Aug. 2007. www.gksoft.com/govt/en/tr.html

"Turkey Sets the Standard on Helping Street Children." *Turkish Daily News*. 29 June 2006. 8 Aug. 2007. www.turkishdailynews.com.tr/article.php?enewsid=47386

"Turkish Economy." GeoInvestor.com. 9 Aug. 2007. www.geoinvestor.com/statistics/turkey/economicdata.htm

"Turkey's Economy Soars." *The Banker*. 2 May 2005. 9 Aug. 2007. www.thebanker.com/news/categoryfront.php/id/443/Turkey's_Economy_Soars.html

United States Central Intelligence Agency. *The World Factbook—Turkey*. 19 July 2007. 9 Aug. 2007. https://www.cia.gov/library/publications/the-world-factbook/geos/tu.html

United States Library of Congress. Federal Research Division. "A Country Study: Turkey." Ed. Helen Chapin Metz. January 1995. 8 Aug. 2007. http://lcweb2.loc.gov/frd/cs/trtoc.html

White, Jenny B. "Two Weddings." *Everyday Life in the Muslim Middle East*. 2nd ed. Eds. Donna Lee Bowen and Evelyn A. Early. Bloomington: Indiana University Press, 2002.

Zürcher, Erik. *Turkey: A Modern History*. London, England: I. B. Tauris, 2004.

Index

About the Author
Alexandra Lilly

Alexandra Lilly has been writing for more than 30 years. She has written newspaper and magazine articles, video scripts, and books for children. She enjoys writing about history, science, and geography. Lilly lives with her husband in South Carolina.

About the Content Adviser
David C. Cuthell, Ph.D.

A scholar of international and public affairs, Dr. David C. Cuthell serves as the director of the Institute of Turkish Studies in Washington, D.C. Cuthell grew up in Istanbul, Turkey. He has an interest in the history of Turkey and has taught at Stevens Institute of Technology in New Jersey, Columbia University in New York, and Georgetown University in Washington, D.C.